Year
of
The White Tiger

Tim and Regina Gort

Two Timbers Press

Gwinn, Michigan

Foreward

> "...the fate of poetry is to fall in love with the world, in
> spite of history."
>
> -Derek Walcott

These poems were not written in leisure, not born out of want, but of necessity. A reasonable urgency I sense few poets today write with. How do we live in this world when it's marked with hardship? How do we love in this world when we're full of grief?

Regina and Tim Gort, the two poets whose hearts and minds are present in the writing of Year of the White Tiger, are husband and wife struggling through such questions together.

This is a rare collection, deep in emotion, rich with imagery both wild and domestic, and magnificently textured with voice. Unlike most books of poems out there, in Year of the White Tiger we have the crystallization of two broken voices uniting. Finding their way alone and then being found within the other. There are poems in this book written by Regina (signaled by Italics) and poems written by Tim (in Bold), and then, what's remarkable, is that the two distinctly identifiable voices somehow become a singular, clear voice with a lasting echo of each (Bold and Italics). I believe this particular passage is immaculate:

> Two voices, infinite sounds,
> shattering syllables like
> teacups on a sunlit porch
> surrounded by ivory walls.

Oftentimes in this volume we're faced with the question of beginnings. Most of which: the beginning of sorrow. What's at the core of this book is a grave misfortune, a very troubled parenthood. It's no delicate thing, losing a daughter still in the womb (Gabrielle Sophia, "Twin B"). It's no small measure, beyond that despair, to parent three children, two with special needs—Gwendolyn ("Twin A," who was born with these qualities) and Eliza, born several years later (who, though born without them, was mistreated shortly after birth, an error by the hospital resulting in such qualities similar to Gwendolyn's). Of the three born to this world, Violet is their only daughter without these limiting qualities. We sense the gravity when we come upon a passage such as, "He compresses his sorrow/ before walking across the lot,/ back to his office building." The "compression of sorrow!" Isn't this true of the feeling of post-traumatic-stress disorder?

I respect and admire the Gort's ability to sit with and honor their history, how they are able to fall in love with the world despite their grievances. This comes, I think, only through meditation. Theirs is a life they did not choose, but are willing to embrace. "For every cursed step, we found/ softness." What's delivered throughout are poems that fill the space among "stars born/ between heart-beats."

This book is a testament to the resilience of the human spirit, the solace found in nature, and the importance of poetry. How it is that our attention given is "a reflection of love," and how that love is essential to live by. The tension between self-preservation and compassion is stunning. Thank goodness, the Gort's get it: art is salvation; that, "… the moment gets stitched up/ into the whole of it all/ if I don't put pen to paper."

Just as these are poems that had to be written, this is a book that must be read. You won't find these emotional truths elsewhere. Sit with them. Notice, as someone once told me, how the power of stillness is a source of gathering.

-Z.G. Tomaszewski

For our daughters, Gwendolyn, Violet and Eliza,
and for their sister Gabrielle Sophia

"How do you value your life if
you only measure it by time?"
-Nessa McCasey, PTP, CPT, Mentor

Authors' Note:

Bold type denotes Tim's writing

Italic type denotes Regina's writing

Bold and Italic type denotes when Regina and Tim write as one

Contents

earth

We bid farewell to our daughters

There is time before I go
to mention the purple and white, sometimes pink,
forget-me-knots down the two-track road.
How when they are so abundant
they go missing after a while.
I'm speaking now of noticing
how little is powerful.

There is time before I go
to mention the curl of fiddleheads,
how when they unfurl their poison multiplies.
I'm speaking now of self-preservation.

There is time to tell you the only story
we know, a father and mother set out
across billion-year-old cliffs, through gales. Man and woman
become the children they always were.

There is time before we go to show you
the way to the riverbed
where we yank ramps for breakfast, to show you
the way past the trout lilies, beneath the raspberry
brambles and hemlock branches
where after the flood we bed down
into threads of silt.

Stillness
(After Tishani Doshi)

All morning I try to hold it,
the point of morning
breaking.
It opens with each child's eyelids.

It's the shuffle,
the drawstring pulled
to the dawn light on the grass
the brown rabbit at the driveway's edge
the robins already working.

There is movement on the riverbed,
geese overhead. I only want
to remember the breaths taken
before movement in the house.

I only want to be here for the opening
of yellow tulips on the kitchen table.

Isn't this what you have been trying to capture for so long?
The art of sitting.

For isn't stillness really just attention, a reflection of love.

Graceland Memorial Garden

There, along Interstate 96
as you head northwest
is an office park.

A speckle of buildings and company logos nearly hide
a funeral home entrance amidst the parking sprawl.

There, east towers of an incinerator,
a mausoleum and memorial garden behind flag rows,
a scatter of flat headstones mark soldiers' places.

Under white pines, near a few maples,
a parcel of cedar trees provide a scented trail
to a lost father who visits his child before work.

There, rests a daughter, whose feet were not flat
like her mothers, but arched like his.
He remembers how when pink toes lay
cupped together, they are slippers.

He compresses his sorrow
before walking across the lot,
back to his office building.

There, he sits at a desk,
stares into the woods and pretends
to pump words from a keyboard.

Savor

How quickly I forget the eagle
circling on thermals above my head
backlit by the sun.

How I dismiss the breakdown,
the tears spilled into rain puddles.

How I had to steady myself
on a tree stump to keep
from falling to my knees
as I claimed the tree roots as my bones.

I can barely remember
the blueberry field
on an open sky day,
blue cascading into buckets I held
as my daughter collected pinecones, moss, ferns.

How when two crossbills sit at the feeder, red underbellies glistening, and
laughter pours out onto me,
the moment gets stitched up
into the whole of it all
if I don't put pen to paper.

How I must savor these times
where only the two of us exist,
like opening the sack of chanterelles he brought home.

wood

Target
(After William Stafford)

It started before your grandparent's children
robbed graves to come to the New World.
It started before Rudy dug a foundation on Lake Superior, where his heart
gave out from heaving sandstone.

Before Maxine delivered your mother, before she gave up
her second and labored four more.
Before Ruth birthed two girls,
claimed the land and held it between them.

Before clergy cast you into guilt-ridden. Even your grandparents
knew that bastards were everywhere.
Before the eldest gutted her first trout. Before the youngest broke her knee.

Before farmers struck into clay and piled
rocks around a maple tree abandoned in the field.
You were aimed even before Nicholas drove
an eighteen-wheeler across the island
for payment in rice and beans.

Before the waters washed us down,
to a four-corner stoplight and a little
church for the poor.
Before Lucilla grafted a lime branch to a lemon tree,
and Juan chased the sugarcane train, stood on the beach
watching others swim.

You were aimed from the beginning, toward the
trees' mossy crowns,
spun from hand-me-down sweaters
you insist you'll never wear.

Poetry is a house

For William Stafford
(After "One Home")

Ours is a North Coast home—a house we share.
Sandstone shoes walk the thoughts that make our creed.
We dance to made-up songs;
the floor is our table.

The hand-made jam labels
we paste on mason jars
mark the dates we store in cupboards-
outside, the Indian paintbrushes
and pine grosbeaks in the morning.

A mother black bear lunged at us
in a September dusk while we
were creek-water sneaking before
our children pulled a blanket
of Northern Lights overhead.

To anyone who looks at us
we say "Come in";
liking the ax handle of invitation,
we could say "Welcome."
(But sandstone shoes walk the thoughts that make our creed.)

The sunrise over Superior
is the tooth of a saw.
Circling our arms we swim
against the north winds.

One became many

One became many, many into a swarm
a hum inside the living room wall,
a hole outside through the brown-vinyl siding
where they staged on the windowsill
darting past foxglove and phlox,
taking pit stops at the hummingbird feeder.

I daydreamed of a honey-filled wall
like in that church your friend owned.

Two stories of honeycomb scraped
from the white wooden slats where I stroked
my pregnant belly in stained-glass, honey dripping down
on us like prayers.

You said it wasn't possible, not another chance.
It couldn't be bees again.
You wanted to spray without proof.

And even after the beekeeper came
and even though the bees
were not bees, but wasps
what makes them of less value to us.

Now, inside, the wall is silent, outside, the hole is patched.

It's hard to say when it all started

It could have been the first time you smiled at me, asked me to take my coat, get me a cup of coffee or tea.

It may have been when you ordered chicken-fried steak at Casey Stengel's or when you told me you liked to read Whitman.

It could have been when you shared with me your signature phrase "Love, luck and lollipops."

It may have been during our AOL instant message exchanges, where you hid behind nothing and pressed computer keys into my heart.

It might have been all or none of these times.

It seems like we were both so different then, when we began this life of fantastical love and ghastly truth.

Before we began to unveil the layers, our knees were always skinned. We were summer children running on sidewalks.

Little did you or I know that the bits of light we had then would grow into stars born between heart-beats where we fill the spaces between.

fire

How to start a fire in the rain

(After Margaret Atwood)

Marriage is
learning to make
fire when the
wind howls along
at 30 knots and the
rain peels down
against your cold,
shaky hands. They rattle
the last match to cardboard
falling apart. Inside
the teepee of maple
and birch bark kindling,
the wood leans
on itself.

Just as you
strike and
zip onto the
red tip,
everything crumbles.
Until upon
your heavy breath, a
hand touches your
shoulder, hands you a
dry box filled
with a truth
higher than the
day before that
has nothing to
do with fire or rain
or survival.

Light cultivar

We're paper suns folded from ferns
hurling through the heavens.
We plunge our fiery bodies
into the seabed, a salt-womb

of purple starfish
under an oystercatcher's beak,
carried beyond the cliff
where, we rake in the stars.

Each footstep a sponge
of nebula, each arm thrust
a radiant explosion.

We shock the redwood forest floor
where we ride on the backs of banana slugs,
ascend the scale of notes
released from the hermit thrush's throat.

After the pyre
(with nod and thanks to Li-Young Lee)

It turns out, what keeps you alive as a parent at mid-life is following your child from Isolette caves to surgery rooms to a home at war with a hospital, and any other parent who looks like you, what allows you to pass through scratched-out, yellow-bricked halls, through stations of nurses smiling about the merits of a new children's hospital, 15 floors, brick-by-brick of better medicine by better technology, and doctors thinking they're contenders for Sainthood, and will tell it to your face, coup d'etat to all of the other medical facilities in town, brand-new mothers going home with their children, and pigeons on the burned-out helipad, fire-retardant dried on the windows of the seventh floor where it all came crashing down, the overdosed kid with a tracheostomy that can't be reversed, the doctor who turned a valve the wrong way causing brain-damage - the child who's a perfect sister- to devastated parents in the cancer ward next door, knowing medicine couldn't douse the pyre before it's updraft took their child, a stuffed penguin left behind,
what keeps your children safe even among the others, some like them, some more like you, some numb, some crippled by pain, some barely alive, some always smiling, some never saying a word, tricks you learned to become impervious, knowledge-keeping you perfected, playing nurse, playing doctor, playing devil's advocate, stupid, weak, strong,
playing communications expert, playing student, playing poor-little child, playing Dutch-reformed, playing Methodist, playing caregiver, in love, parent-of-the-year, playing crazy, healthy, blessed, immoral, playing terrified, playing fearless, happy, sad, sleep-deprived, over-caffeinated, puzzled, playing interested, playing bored, playing unfair, playing post-traumatic stress disorder playing "I'm just so blessed with this life," it turns out, now that you're old nearing the dawn of a new life,

what kept you alive all that time never let you fully live.

Morning

Outside, the season's first
ship leaves Duluth, a tug sheaving
a sea of endless ice under
a grey sky, a bright pilot house
against the always dark.

Winter storms shout down
as the sun's light, a distant memory in the pine quiet,
waits in a chorus of white.

We wait, too, in silent
appreciation - a good suffering we say.

Inside, the fire draws
into the flue, speaking in tongues:
the birch bark smacks, finger-flecks
crack pine, maplewood whistles
to a smoky bellow.

Wind against a sandstone chimney is love: what was
and what is no longer here. A frosty morning, the coals coax us
from our lake-slumber, a saucer-pan
night of dreams, where we swim into blue-green,
over reefs and under folding waves.

We, viscous shards of light,
even the Aleutian winds
skimming the cliffs
do not reduce our wildness.
We thrust our bodies streamline,
mouths wide open at the surface.

On our island, the conifers are alarm clocks,
just before the Raven croaks us into song.

water

Post-traumatic-stress disorder

With blue jeans rolled up,
you enter unwillingly, can't
help it.

It's too deep.

From the outside, the
current barely moves.
But the moving weight numbs
you, not all you, only parts.

How could you not move with
it; it measures you like
fishermen drowning in
wonder.

Its winding murk, its
unconscious slouching like
preserved leaves circling from
the bottom heap. The sand
never settling, always
rising from under what's
sunk below.

You try to grasp, dig your toes in,
chase each spring-gush and pebble-slip
past the tad-poles and trout.

You become too familiar with
the flood, but eventually
turn from silt into
sun-cracked, mud-shine.

You know tributaries must
be related to tribes.

Lake trout
(After David Whyte)

For too many days I have not seen
Lake Superior, nor the streams,
nor the long-shore currents
between Picnic Rocks.

For too many nights I have not imagined
the lake trout staging at the
river-mouth as snowmelt rushes on,
nor have I dreamed of her desire,
the jack-knifing of her
tail toward sand and rock.

I have not given myself up to her depth,
the dark bottom of the lake,
nor the grand openness of water
to the north, the east, the west,
nor the storms she endures beneath the cigar-tip-moon.

I have not felt the heaving forth of the Great Saltless Sea, the
symphonic cymbal crashing, its white arms lifting, pulling wind
past breath, heavy and cold.

I have not heard those waves fallen from clouds
into the world, pearling granite into sands.

Superior is in me,
the northern lights dance, and I am ready
like the little lake trout to leave her stream,
driven by hunger, guided by stars,
as she empties herself into clear water.

How to fight

I hoist a warning flag, a red one
flapping in the north wind
barreling across Rock Beach.

Avoid the spewing rip currents
from my mouth.

You are one foot anchor
in a shifting sandbar,
two arm strokes from struggle,
I may let you bob
before pulling you under.

I'm drawn to danger,
damn near live
for the line between
control and out.

Currents call me,
weightless on your energy,
I force my tongue-not hold it.

Word storms endure.

The clouds open
as a child's needs.

We reflect on joint tasks,
our hands and breath
meet in thrash and rock.

How to love someone

You will never embrace him
like a wave, the foam bed is without you.
It's where he rests after
he's squared his shoulders, squatted his legs,
pumping, pumping, pumping.

You'll never come between him
and the waves:
This is more than an affair, more than a mistress. On his death bed
his mouth will be salty.
You will swab his lips with your tongue
and the water will remind him
of his first barrel, his first time
the wave pounded him into the sand
breaking the air from his lungs.

You must accept the muse
until your ashes are ushered
into the flowing causeway
where he rides.

You will never bridge her
like the rope she throws overhead,
the pink rainbow echoing with each whip,
each step-up, a bead of sweat
dropping for every shuffle-jump,
spin, jump, cradle.

You will never come between her
and the ring where weighted ropes bond her,
and where she floats on
blue-peach tennis shoes.

She pushes her lungs past
the smell of leather gloves,
Hoe-ha! Hoe-ha! as the bag dances
to her momentum, the floor creaking
with each swing, her ancestors,
her zen-state, her art-form, throwing
and learning to be thrown - to take one.

On her death bed her lip
will be cold but curled, just slightly
in the corner from all of those uppercuts, jabs
and hooks. And from her breathing,
blow by blow by blow.

Marriage

It's the back cast
back-and-forth
of your smile that ties me up
like white-deer-belly hair
on a hook. We tangle in a whisper-spun line
of twins conceived in a Memphis hotel.

We claim the riverbed 'til the backward
snap of a wrist snags me.

Gutted, I spill spawn
onto a sterile table.

Twin A: alive.
Twin B: still.

If not
(After Julie Hanson)

This will remind you of the tent
slanting against a sphagnum covered hill.
If not, a moon will.

This will remind you of swans
trumpeting on an inland lake
while our tent heats in the morning.
If not, frost will.

This will remind you of floating
on your back, in an icy riverbed.
If not, my hands will.

This will remind you of two brown pelicans
rising out of Pacific fog.
If not, humidity will.

This will remind you of the barred owl
who played leapfrog in the pines.
If not, the rain will.

This will remind you of Smuggler's Cove,
acorn barnacles cemented on rocks.
If not, the tide will.

This will remind you of the steelhead
green river where you cried, when I held you.
If not, this poem will.

air

Pregnant again

This time he doesn't use me,
my taut belly, a canvas,
doesn't splatter egg-yolk
tempura across my skin.

This time I don't fold
layettes into stacks
tucked into drawers with white booties,
darned woolen caps and quilted-patch blankets.

This time we don't say the name.
This time we don't sing rock-a-bye.

This time you drink dark coffee, imported beer,
smoke cigars in the garden shed.
This time I eat mint ice cream, curly fries
and let my prayers hang between us.

When two moons smile

If you as one are possible,
strong even, then you plus him
is so much more, invincible maybe.

If you as one are vulnerable
then you plus her
are a heart blown through.

Two voices, infinite sounds,
shattering syllables like
teacups on a sunlit porch
surrounded by ivory walls.

If we as one are written
jointly, then morning quarrels
amoung bed sheets and coos,
become slick, pliable even.

This word
(For Etheridge Knight)

And this word.
This word.
This word is a bubble of air.
A chest compression.
And a flat line.

A long, silent pause for the sufferers.
A still moving picture that cannot be shared
because these kinds of steps are new.

For those who wait in recovery rooms
For those who are looking for answers on monitors
For those who are too afraid to talk
For young Eliza Madeline

A vidid infant
A tiny warrior who overcame the odds,
showed us who she was before
anyone hardly knew her name:
The White Tiger from a jinx.

This moving.
And this moving.
This moving through blood and bile and shit.
The American healthcare system.
For Eliza who is a song and a stone
and feather of feeling.
Now alive and here. Right here,
In her day.

This word is a bluejay feather,
Red, wet clay, an earthly
Buddha shining over
the silvery siltstone
riverbeds breathing up
from the mud.

For our first
kiss by Superior
For Sterling and Ruth and a Sunday walk
to the Little Garlic and back,
her father and mother's house along the lake
For Jan and Jim
love too far
from home. Love too far
from the day everyone remembers. Everyone
sings. Everyone sings. We sing.

Maybe

Maybe my shadow feet
beneath yards of tulle predicted
our union as doomed.

Maybe the wedding photos
snapped as you and I leaned
under a crypt. A rose bouquet draped
over headstones, foretold our loss.

Maybe it was the ultrasound
cast over twins, when one's heart
wouldn't flow, that fated us to grief.

Maybe it was seeing my breaking point
in you, my yarn unspun
a long time before
shuffling our bronze feet slowly,
our shadows cast outlines in snow.

For every cursed step, we found
softness: a finger, a kiss, a
whisper, a meditation in a
poem.

Maybe from need, the sea
swallowed you, the earth
hid me, waiting for
fire and wind to come.

Maybe we travel without
maps, get lost in tracks,
guide one another through
a jagged course.

Maybe our veins
run blue from morning baths,
the lake's edge holding our
naked bodies warmed by
sun-heated sandstone.

The remains
(After Mark Strand)

We empty ourselves of the names
of doctors, of nurses, surgeons and social workers.

We empty ourselves of the names
of lawyers, of insurance companies, of judges,
a courtroom reporter who cries as she tick-taps.

We empty ourselves of the yellow-brick house,
the beds of pink peonies and the two sugar maples
we transplanted. We empty ourselves
of the people we were, aspired to be,
who once adopted a dog
and returned it the next day.

We empty ourselves of the family,
the father and mother we thought
we'd become. Now empty
we fill ourselves with lies, truths
and what's blurred between,
until we right our way
with words. We fill ourselves
with tamarack water, a grey canoe,
an eastern breeze on black dragonfly wings,
Great Blue Heron, an elder statesman,
our river bend guide.

We fill ourselves with lichen mounds,
a red pocket knife and green cloth bag,
clutched close.

We fill ourselves with a whispered mantra, wafts of sage smoke,
a candle's flame as we inhale, as we exhale.

Now full, we empty ourselves again.

with thanks

Thanks to the editors of *North Dakota Quarterly* for publishing Regina and Tim's first collaborative poem, "Poetry is a House".

Regina greatly appreciates the love and support from the Literary Giants, Cynthia and Amanda, Juliet and Kathy, Rebecca and The Schuler Books writing group, Roni and the Literary Life, Deb and Ann, Joanne and Karen and Oubria in the Heartland, Helen and the Joy Center, Marquette Poets Circle, brave Tricia, Kelly, Andrea, always Zachary, her family and hours spent foraging, finding, seeking, relishing. With thanks most especially to my love, Tim, for writing life with me.

Tim is thankful to the Cascade Writers Group, which gave him courage to write, edit and share, to Nessa McCasey, to Jamison and Pete, to Bill and Russ, to the rest of his family (with bloodlines and to the many without), to Zachary for partnering in poetry and on foot through mountains, streams and lakes, to the strange gurus who test his patience on and off the roads of America, and to the Northwoods for providing an inspiring backdrop to live and write an amazing life. To my love, Regina, for constantly encouraging me to let my feet float from an always-shifting ground.

With special thanks to Becky Pelky and Timston.